Stories of Colonial Times

Susan Ring · Illustrated by Kate McKeon

Contents

Rigby

A Harcourt Achieve Imprint

www.Rigby.com
1-800-531-5015

WHAT CHEER!

Long ago, before there was a country called the United States or even a place called America, a 12-year-old boy named Moattoqus (mo-AT-o-kus) lived at the edge of a large, dark forest. He and his family were part of the Narragansett tribe who lived in the area along the Atlantic Ocean that would one day become the state of Rhode Island.

Moattoqus's name meant Black Wolf, and he was very strong and brave. While his brothers were afraid to enter the dark and eerie forest, which was full of savage beasts and poisonous creatures, brave Moattoqus was not afraid to explore the spooky woods. He entered the forest each morning at sunrise and would remain there until he gathered enough food for his family's evening feast.

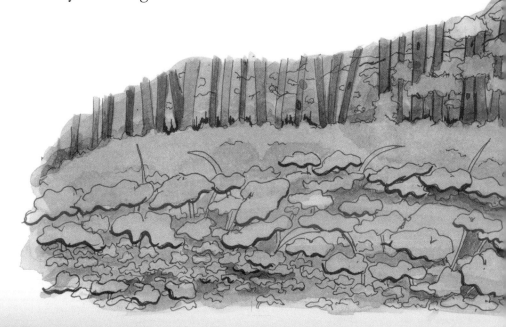

One morning Moattoqus entered the dimly lit forest in his search for food. As he was exploring the area, he noticed a strange light coming from the depths of the woods. Moattoqus inched closer and closer but could not determine the source of the small flickering light. As he moved closer, he discovered that the light was coming from a small lantern that was lying on a patch of soggy ground.

Moattoqus examined the tiny yellow flame that was beginning to fade inside the lantern. This was not a tool that the Narragansett tribe used. It must have belonged to one of the English colonists.

Moattoqus had heard stories about the white-skinned people in their long, heavy coats who had settled in the area, but he had never seen one up close. He'd heard that these people would trade things with the Narragansett, but he'd also heard stories about them taking his people away. Moattoqus wondered if the person who had left this lantern behind was a friend or an enemy.

Just then, a scream echoed through the forest. "Help! Someone help me!"

Moattoqus knew exactly where that scream had come from—the bottom of a trap hole!

Some weeks ago, Moattoqus had dug a deep hole in the ground as a trap for animals. This was one way that he gathered food for his family. The top was covered with sticks and leaves so it was hidden. Someone must have fallen inside!

Moattoqus raced to the hole where he stumbled upon a young colonist trapped at the bottom. The boy's face was cut, and his clothes were badly torn. He peered up at Moattoqus while cradling his arm close to his chest.

"Help . . . please!" cried the boy. "My name is Daniel Williams! My father is Roger Williams . . . he is the leader of the colony over the next hill. Please help me! I . . . I think I may have broken my arm!"

Moattoqus did not understand what the boy was saying since he did not speak the same language. Even so, he knew that he should help the wounded boy.

Lowering himself to the ground, Moattoqus stretched out his arm as far as he could. At first Daniel stared at him, not sure if Moattoqus meant to help him or hurt him. After a moment Daniel reached up to Moattoqus's hand.

"I . . . I can't reach," Daniel said weakly.

Moattoqus stood up and searched the area for something he could use to pull Daniel out of the hole. He found a long branch, but because of his broken arm, Daniel could barely grab hold of it.

Moattoqus found a thick vine that he lowered down to Daniel. He then pretended to tie the vine around his waist. Daniel understood—Moattoqus wanted him to tie the vine around his waist so he could pull him up.

Daniel tied the vine around his waist, and Moattoqus began pulling with all his strength. As he pulled, however, he slid closer to the edge of the hole. The ground was soft and wet, and before Moattoqus could do anything, the ground had given way below him and he tumbled down into the hole, too!

Moattoqus and Daniel sank down to the ground, feeling helpless and afraid. Now they were both trapped. Would anyone come looking for them?

"Why did I explore the forest all by myself?" Daniel asked quietly. "What if I never see my family again?"

The two boys stared at each other with curiosity. Finally, Moattoqus pointed at Daniel and said, "Neetop." *Neetop* was the Narragansett word for *friend*.

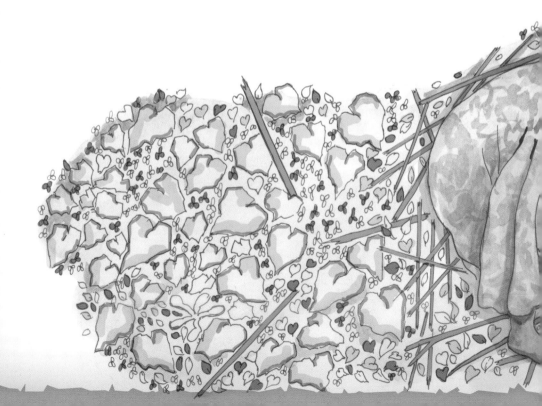

Daniel pointed at himself and asked, "Neetop?" Moattoqus smiled and nodded his head, so Daniel pointed back at him and said, "Neetop."

"What cheer, Neetop?" came a man's voice from above.

There were two dark shapes staring down into the hole. The boys cowered together until Daniel peered up and saw who it was that had spoken.

"Father!" Daniel cried happily.

Then, Moattoqus recognized the other figure.

"Father!" Moattoqus said in English, laughing.

Roger Williams and Moattoqus's father Canonicus had been in a meeting of friendship and goodwill when they realized that their boys were missing. Canonicus guessed that his son was probably hunting in the forest, and Roger had known that his son was going to spend the day exploring. It was easy to guess what had happened.

Roger and Canonicus were good friends and had learned each other's languages. Most colonists would never use a Narragansett greeting, but Roger showed respect and kindness to Canonicus and his people.

Together, the two men had worked to make the English settlement a success. Without the help of the Narragansett tribe, the Rhode Island colony would have failed.

After rescuing the boys from the hole, Roger inspected his son's arm and determined that it was only sprained and not broken.

Roger wanted to thank Moattoqus for everything he had done for his son. He reached into his coat pocket and pulled out a metal spoon and a pewter cup. They were made in England, miles and miles away. Moattoqus had never seen anything like them.

"Say *thank you*," Canonicus said, pronouncing the English words carefully for his son.

Moattoqus sounded the words out in his mind and then said, "Thank you."

"What cheer, Neetop?" Daniel asked, which was his way of saying, "What's up, my friend?"

Moattoqus sounded these words out in his mind as well and then repeated them. "What cheer, Neetop?"

TALES OF LONG AGO

As told to Susan Ring by John McNiff

My name is John McNiff and I'm a park ranger at the Roger Williams National Memorial in Providence, Rhode Island. The park was established in honor of Roger Williams, the founder of Providence, Rhode Island. It is located on the land Williams originally claimed for his **colony**. The park is only 4.5 **acres,** making it one of the smallest national parks in the country.

Even though the park itself is small, the stories it holds are huge! I enjoy telling visitors all about Roger Williams and the Narragansett tribe who originally lived in the area.

This statue of Roger Williams stands in Providence, Rhode Island.

ROGER WILLIAMS

Roger Williams was born in England on December 21, 1603. Even though Williams spent his early life in England, he was unhappy there because he did not have the freedom to express his beliefs about religion. To gain this freedom, he and his wife Mary set sail for the Massachusetts Bay Colony in 1630. They arrived at the colony on February 5, 1631.

Roger Williams and his wife first lived in the Massachusetts Bay Colony.

Unfortunately, Williams did not find the freedom he was looking for in Massachusetts. Eventually, he bought land from his Native American friends, the Narragansett, to establish a new colony, Providence, as a place where everyone would have religious freedom.

Providence, Rhode Island

I am very enthusiastic about Roger Williams's life and his struggle for religious freedom, so I try to help park visitors understand that he was a real person. In fact, he was actually considered by some to be an outlaw in his day. Several times he was forced to move away from a town because of his **rebellious** beliefs. At other times he was put on trial for his opinions, which others found dangerous.

He also formed close bonds with the Narragansett by learning their language and customs. This led to his urging the King of England to stop taking their land. He explained that the Native Americans needed it to survive. Again, this idea made him very unpopular with his fellow **colonists** and the government.

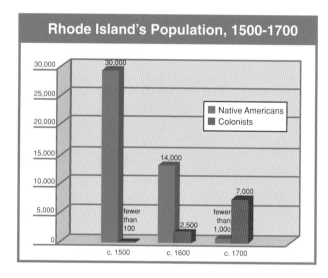

Rhode Island's Population, 1500-1700

	Native Americans	Colonists
c. 1500	30,000	fewer than 100
c. 1600	14,000	2,500
c. 1700	fewer than 1,000	7,000

Roger Williams made friends with the Narragansett and fought to help them keep their land.

When I'm not telling tales about Roger, I show visitors around our small park. It's an interesting place that makes history meaningful to today's visitors. We have some fascinating old documents signed by Roger Williams and a compass and sundial that once belonged to him. The small landmark building is filled with other interesting artifacts from early America, both Native Americans and colonists.

What Time Is It?

A sundial tells time using the position of the sun in the sky. The sun casts a shadow on the sundial's surface, which is marked with the hours of the day. As the position of the sun changes, the time indicated by the shadow changes.

Roger Williams's sundial

SHARING STORIES IN SCHOOLS

Working at the park is a big part of my job, but I also go to schools and talk to students about Rhode Island before the colonists arrived and settled the area.

"Can you imagine," I ask the students, "a time when there were no cars, no electricity, no airports or office buildings? There weren't even schools! It was a time before the colonists arrived, and only Native American people lived on the land in this area."

I enjoy telling kids about the Native Americans who lived in this area by introducing them to the native language and the meaning of certain words. For example, the Wampanoag people lived furthest east along the Atlantic coast, so their name means "people of the first light" because the sun rises in the east. The Nipmuc people didn't live near the salty ocean, so their name means "fresh water people."

I also teach kids the phrase "What Cheer, Neetop?" That was a common greeting in the Narragansett language. It means, *what's up, my friend?*

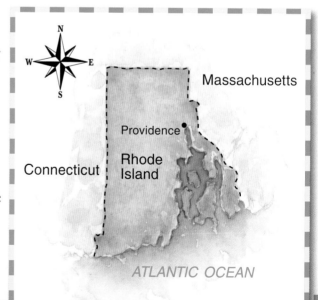

Native Americans made canoes out of many natural materials. Today canoes are made out of plastic or fiberglass.

I tell the students how the Native Americans caught whales and other animals. I also show them how Native Americans used other animals such as deer and moose for clothing and food and even how they made tools out of antlers. Everything on the animals they hunted was used for survival.

The Narragansett used canoes to travel on water, so I tell students about the canoes that they paddled along the rivers and ocean. The students can't believe it when I tell them that about 40 people could fit into each Narragansett canoe! Today, canoes are made from fiberglass or some other type of plastic material, but Narragansett canoes were made out of one whole tree, usually a chestnut tree.

MANY WAYS TO TELL A STORY

I like to use many different things to make the stories of long ago have meaning for students because the stories I tell are about real people and real events. People who lived in the 17th Century had many of the same needs that people do today, such as food, clothing, and shelter.

Colonial Cabin

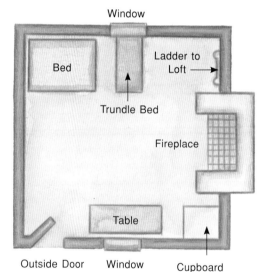

Window

Bed

Ladder to Loft →

Trundle Bed

Fireplace

Table

Outside Door   Window   Cupboard

Modern House

Bath   Bedroom

Kitchen

Dining Room   Living Room

In colonial times, people often lived in one room cabins which were heated by a fireplace. Today, houses have many rooms and modern features.

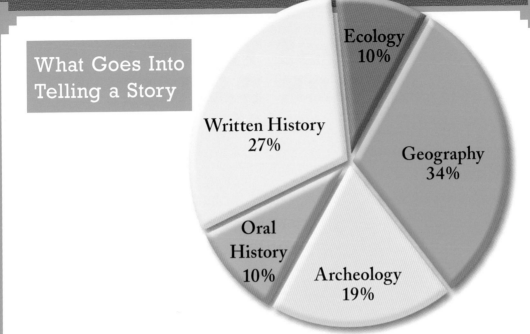

What Goes Into Telling a Story

Ecology 10%

Written History 27%

Geography 34%

Oral History 10%

Archeology 19%

I use many different subject areas to tell stories. I use **archeology** by showing real tools, weapons, and canteens that were typical of the time. I also use real written historical documents to tell stories that have been passed down by Native Americans over the years.

I also use **geography** by presenting old maps of towns and villages. One of my favorite games to play in the classroom uses a huge map of southern New England. I like to use the large map to teach about history, and the people that lived here so long ago. I place the canvas map on the floor and have students move around on it to give them a better understanding of the travels of people in colonial times.

Even the **ecology** of an area helps tell the story. Looking at the plants and animals native to the area and discussing how they were used gives a fuller picture of how life was lived.

MORE THAN A PARK RANGER

On my days off from being a park ranger, I like to tell stories about pirates! I have been teaching kids about pirates for about ten years.

Did you know that pirates actually had a set of laws that they followed on the ships? It's true! Before boarding the ship, each crew member signed an **article** that stated the rules and each person's job. They also voted on what would happen on the pirate ships. Anyone who was a member of the crew had a say, and they could all agree to vote off the captain if they desired. In fact, the way the pirates governed themselves led to the creation of an important U.S. historical document, the Articles of Confederation.

The way pirates governed their ships led to the U.S. Articles of Confederation.

I have so many incredible stories about pirates, colonists, Native Americans, and Roger Williams that I would like to share by either visiting schools, talking with visitors, or writing books and articles. For example, I want to write a story about how Roger Williams and William Shakespeare, the famous playwright, knew each other. Now that would be an amazing book!

But for now, I will continue to tell the stories of colonial times at my park and at local schools. Come visit me sometime!

Park rangers know many fascinating things about their parks.

GLOSSARY

acre an area of land that is equal to 43,560 square feet

archeology the study of the remains of past life

article an important historical document or a story in a magazine

colony a settlement built by and ruled by people from another country

colonist someone who lives in a colony

ecology the study of organisms and their environment

geography the study of the earth's surface, physical features and their locations

rebellious to act in a way opposite of rules and authority